Habry

or

The End Of Snow

poems by

Helen Degen Cohen

The Puddin'head Press
2009

Additional copies of this book
may be ordered by writing to:

The Puddin'head Press
PO Box 477889
Chicago IL 60647
708-656-4900

www.puddinheadpress.com

All rights reserved. No part of this book
may be reproduced in any manner
(except brief quotations for review purposes)
without the written permission of the author.

Cover design by Helen Degen Cohen

First Edition
2009

ISBN# 978-0-9819756-0-3

Copyright 2009
By Helen Degen Cohen

for

Joseph and Bella

and Maria Szumska

Acknowledgements

Grateful acknowledgement is made to the following publications, in whose pages these poems first appeared, at times in a slightly different form:

"The End Of Snow" in *After Hours;* "The Faces, Up There" in ***The Antigonish Review* (Canada);** Polish translations of "Habry", "Hair", "Lord, There Is Something", "Ruda Felka", and "That dark golden Jewish light" in ***Akcent* (Poland);** "The Trains" in ***Ascent;*** "I remember coming into Warsaw, a child" (first prize, *Soundings*), "In Hiding", "The Prison As A Gray Box", and "Sing Illinois" in ***Concert at Chopin's House: A Collection of Polish-American Writing;*** "Retirement Village" and "The Village Girl's Dream" in *Korone;* "Glass Beaded Rings" in ***Outerbridge;*** "Light" in ***The Partisan Review;*** "Balalaika", "The Chorus… Variations On A Theme", "The Return Of Rhyme", "Snow Is Falling On The Underground", "The War Gave Birth To Me", and "The Woman With Many Lines" in ***Rhino;*** "I have been lost in an image forest" in ***Scintillations II*** (first prize); "Habry", "Ruda Felka" (English), and "Survivors" in *Shofar;* "My Mother's Dishes" in ***Something of My Very Own To Say – American Women Writers of Polish Descent* (Columbia University Press);** "And The Airplanes Fly", "And The Snow Kept Falling", "So Many Parades, Mirenka", "The Star In The Window Is Yellow", and "The War" in ***Spoon River Quarterly's feature, SRQ Illinois Poet Helen Degen Cohen;*** "A View From The Ghetto" in ***Stand Magazine* (England);** "My Mother's Roots" in ***Where We Find Ourselves - Jewish Women Around the World Write about Home* (SUNY).**

The author would like to thank the following foundations where, over a period of time, some of this work was created or revised: Yaddo, The MacDowell Colony, The Virginia Center for the Creative Arts, and especially Ragdale for many productive stays there. And to my publisher whose wild grape wine is the best anywhere.

Work on these poems was made possible in part by grants from The National Endowment for the Arts and The Illinois Arts Council.

Table Of Contents

The End of Snow	1
The Chorus… Variations On A Theme	5
Snow Is Falling On The Underground	6
The War	8
The Star In The Window Is Yellow	10
Lord, There Is Something	11
Ruda Felka	12
Hair	14
And The Snow Kept Falling	16
That dark golden Jewish light	19
I have been lost in an image forest	20
A View From The Ghetto	21
So Many Parades, Mirenka	22
Glass Beaded Rings	24
Light	26
The Prison As A Gray Box	28
Balalaika	30
Joseph's Ark	31
And The Airplanes Fly	32
The Trains	33
In Hiding	34
Haloes	36
Joseph On The Night Of Nights	38
The Village Girl's Dream	40
Habry	39

I remember coming into Warsaw, a child	45
The Children of War Smile And Are Happy	46
Sing Illinois	48
The War Gave Birth To Me	50
My Mother's Roots	52
There Are Men	55
Drifting Towards You, Malina	57
Among The Unsurvived	60
Retirement Village	62
People Look In	63
My Mother's Dishes	64
When You Finally Marry	67
How You Saved My Life	72
To Keep My Mother Happy	73
The Faces, Up There	74
It's been centuries	76
The Return Of Rhyme	78
She looked among her friends	79
The Writer	80
Survivors	81
This Morning	82
The Woman With Many Lines	83

Habry

or

The End Of Snow

...snowfall, as if even now you were sleeping.

— Paul Celan (tr. Michael Hamburger)

The End of Snow
After reading Anna Swir

1.

1939 and my mother
    is not the town beauty
  my mother is an orange flower the wind
  can move only so much.
     Iron in hand
     she curls
the butcher's wife's hair.

Powerful gypsies come   in   and   out
     whispering secrets   their eyes like bats
   their skirts sweeping the floor of the beauty shop
My mother the flower says nothing but
   dropping her orange hair, smiles.
Oh. Does she know I'm already inside her?

*

My father the Hun stands on a chair
   sword in hand over his customer—Hah!
waving his razor in the air
      like an orchestra conductor, whop! whop!—
killing them with stories.

The customer laughs, You tickle me, Joe.
My father takes off the white sheet
from around the man's neck and—whips it into the air, snap!
   laughing back, What do you think!
everybody knows me here already!

*

Mama, please don't steal the lilacs.
We are only strangers on the sidewalk, Mama.
When I am a woman, with a house and a fence,
Will you steal lilacs from me too?
Mama, please, don't pick their lillies,
In our house they will turn old,
In our house they will overpower us.

2.

1968 and he curses people who spit in the streets
    curses those who will not arrest them
      curses the missing signs on the grass
    that in Europe told him to KEEP OFF!

You know?—Once I saw Hitler in a parade!
Standing on top of my friend's shoulders!
I saw him! Hah!.... It was really something!

Listen, God had fun making the world!
He is probably still laughing at the joke!
I have to make his acquaintance some time!
Shake his hand! Maybe give him a haircut!
I would be the best barber in heaven!

    He is still laughing.
I am still smiling, growing younger by the minute—
      I am seven, six—
        He lifts me onto his shoulders
            quiet under the trees
      the fields flapping under white clouds
        Even if he tore the horizon apart
    with his screaming, he could still reach God.
        I am bringing my father
          back to paradise.

*

She ruined her hands with chemical solutions
humming as she curled their perfect little oceanwaves
painting on their long fragrant fingernails
      smiling up at their tunics and bows
her hands aswim in the poisonous lacquered waves.

3

      Famous Resistance.   Can it be
that in a thicket in the Underground,   in **1943**

she played a wicked game of chess
        with a former Union leader no less
    both in shirts of
            green parachute?

That   out of a tree-stump   he had carved a chessboard
in the moonlight,   just for her
while,   somewhere in the trees,   a mandolin played?

That,   although she blushed   at the way he looked at her
      she won
    calculating every one of her moves—
            and my father

      came bounding out of the trees
           dragged her back to the fire
  and made her dance with him!

Which embarrassed her for all the rest of her life
    and the war be damned?
                            Like owls, we were
                            lucky to be living in the dark

      My father rose up as if into a dream
when the plane came in the middle of the night.

It was snowing
    the softest quietest snow
  One by one   they came out of their holes
        into the whitest midnight on earth
    snow falling around them like a myth.

As if what they had wished for   had a new name.

  And so came to (she reminds him)
 where the parachute landed
       in a tree
   dropping tinned meat, cigarettes... and news.

Beside the small fire   can it be?
    which to God must have appeared like a flower of light
      in the damp forests of the earth
         below

    a Partisan woman leaned back to sing
     a war ballad   and they sang along.

                           Perhaps it can, in **1989.**

    But my father remembers only
      the snow
     that fell so quietly
          into his dream.

The Chorus... Variations On A Theme
A survivor walks among the war hungry

It smelled so good to him, he came closer,
asked questions, licked at the images,
felt his blood, went hunting in my neighborhood for more—
I live among those deprived of war,
the blunted workaday ones
who would never think of planting a garden.

Once I met someone so jealous that he went there.
Only no one knew him, it wasn't the same.
He had gotten so dressed up for the occasion,
wearing his best coffins, so to speak
and no one knew his name, poor man.
No one even knew he was there.

He wants my ghost to introduce him.
While we who were there dance and dance
and plant roses and petunias.
He looks on, silent and dim.
And we feel so sorry for his peaceful kingdom
but then this chorus begins, all of itself....

Snow Is Falling On The Underground
For Joseph and Bella in the Underground

These are biblical times.
You move with the crowd
you have to move with the crowd.

Snow is falling on the horse's head
into his great dead eyes,
falling as they sit gathered together,
in the country of white thanksgiving,
as they watch the body divided
and thrown to the doglike
hunger of the dwindling,
weakening crowd. And the birds overhead
and the child staring at the horse's head
take with them the odor of blood,
the whiteness of snow.

When they saw the horse coming,
led by the forerunners, the scouts,
to some he looked like a god,
while others waited, cold
as kings and queens, frozen
to their chore of receiving.
Yes he said unto them
out of his flat, snowed-over eyes,
I am neither deaf nor dumb nor blind
but I can't understand you,
I am made differently—
and snow kept falling
on their hands, their thighs,
as they cut him up, as they ate,

those who could neither choose nor be chosen,
but moved, just ahead of the enemy behind them
and the bombs descending from
the holiest aspects of height,
like the snow—
it was too cold to wonder about it,
though the wonder lives on.

They ate the horse.
The child whimpered.
And the snow kept falling.
Even into the holes
they had dug for hiding.
To the very far and wide
circumference beyond the world,
which must be the end of the war.

It was as if someone were singing
the same daily song
out of the same buried songbook:
These are biblical times,
this is winter beginning,
these are the days of the
vanishing horses.

The War
After Marguerite Duras

When we said *the war*
when we thought *the war*
it had nothing to do with weapons
or people
or taking sides
or explosions—all that
is forgotten with the first fear—
it had to do with
a darkness
and we couldn't step out of it,
a mystery
much as the fields that fed us,
I who have been there can tell you
that you live in a
narrow, warless passage
and then—
when the war is over, we'll say,
before the war, we will say,
after the war, we say,
we will do this and that—
when the darkness fades,
ah, then we will live,
we say,
closing our eyes.

A darkness, a house
we cannot come out of,
cannot see out of.
Nor even remember
the unboarding of windows—light;
and we had no privacy there,
we could not imagine anyone

in any country
not living with us—our house
was bigger than a continent,
smaller than a cage.
Familiar as
the smell of ammonia,
the grippe.
When the war began,
I heard my sister
brother cousins
lover
mother and father,
say,
staring at the
graceful
movement
of a hand.

The Star In The Window Is Yellow

The star in the window is yellow.
It hangs on a sleeve of heaven
and heaven is static,
heaven is Jewish,
it cannot fly, my child.

Nor will it leave you.
Nor is it bright with angels, no,
heaven is dark,
it is dark with millions
of yellow stars.

Lord, There Is Something

Lord, there is
something in me
that shines—
I will be the butcher's
or the baker's wife!
They watch me dance
and I bring them peace.
O Lord, there is
something in me I miss,
though they hold it
in their open palms,
the men,
they hold it in their
wide open palms.

And the Lord took off his manhood
and said:

Take the woman amongst you
as a bride, children,
let her keep whitening her dress
day and night,
let her keep turning from side to side,
keep the woman amongst you, always,
as a bride.

Lord, there is
something in me
that shines.
I will be the butcher's
or the baker's wife!
I will dance each day
upon their open palms.

Ruda Felka
For my first nursemaid

First, there is sun
a room for three
mother, father, child
the sun finding its way in
under billowing curtains
and through it
the entire world of light
in building blocks
and leafy patterns.
First, there was sun.
And mama, like the sun
coming, going, brightly floating
her burnished mother-hair
whirling, then gone.
Then think darkness, stone
dragging. Then his warm odor
schnappsy breath, fragrant underarms.
First there is the leaving
of the peaceful sun,
playfuk sun, only sun.

The dark child is the world's
brilliant flower.
Why be sorry for the darkness
    inside it?
Like a black pearl.
They don't understand it.
They would like to remove it
their words like scissors and knives.
Or display it, their peculiar
    jewel.

I will not be cut.
I am only a child.
I will not freeze in a golden frame.
I will get up and dance the Krakovianka.
        until they all close their eyes:
Wreath of cornflowers and orange poppies
colored ribbons flying from my shoulders
sleeves white white white
sequined bodice of black velvet—
I will go to the park with *looks like a goat*
Ruda Felka, who lets me
touch the flowers.

Hair
For Joseph and Bella, on the eve of War

That is my pale, orange mother
Crinkling the pert panienka's hair.
Her own, an abandon of warm silk
To and fro. Then it fades away.

Sometimes she braids my hair into circles
And hums, as if ours were a place for humming.
What is it mothers know?
What is she braiding into my hair?

The sun is shining. There's a bird in the window,
There are voices in the street, in our old village, there is
Darkness around us, yet everything is bright,
Stars seem to shine through the very daylight.

My father's hurt eyes come closer,
Closer, he takes me into his arms.
I lie beside the fragrance of his underarm
Hair, his warm, moist turnings, the stars.

Soon I will be almost five years old.
And still, what I know hides behind the star.
So said the gypsy, long ago,
Your father the barber is going to war.

Up and back he walks, to the door.
He carries me on his back, we laugh,
And still, curled in his eyes are ghosts.
He touches my crib, my toes, my ear,

Knowing that without me there will be no world,
No scissors, no long black combs, no hair,
No brown strap to carry the razor
Up and back, up and back.

Up and back, he walks to the door,
The gypsies stirring the hair on the floor

And that is my pale orange mother
Suddenly trying to fade away.
She braids her humming into my hair,
Her silence into my wild hair.

And The Snow Kept Falling
For my sister, who died at the age of two

Deep, deep in
    the glass toy
there lies a river
    warmer than diamonds
and we sit beside it
girls and boys
    we sit in the snowy glass toy—

You lay down in the snow
leaving a human print when you rose,
and the snow kept falling
on the children, on their houses—
on Aunt Vera, who laughed like a movie star
coming in with her Warsaw shoes and chocolates,
on grandmother in her cooking house
folding her twenty children to sleep,
on uncle feeling the oven-tile wall,
letting the warmth reach into his heart,
on Anna the nursemaid, who walked me to the park,
her legs like a goat's, it was summer, yet snow
fell on her freckles, on our braided hair,
on Nathaniel, soon to be sent to Siberia.
The streets were powdered white,
I was sucking an icicle
and the baker came out laughing
his arms high receiving the snow
as if it had just been made by God,
and it fell on the guts in the butcher shop,
on the tunnels where everyone ran to hide
when the planes came humming—

on the Thursday markets in the open square,
and the women who sat on the ground hawking
chickens and cheeses, on me
and my mother holding onto my hand,
and snow fell on the thunder and the flowers under it—
onto the schnapps in my father's hand,
and the card players humming
La Dona è Mobile, and on David and Rachel,
who were dancing the tango
in the middle of the living room,
Rachel, so modern no snow could reach her,
David, so smooth, that there was no snow—

The streets were already white,
whiter than the page I write on,
and it fell on grandfather rocking in prayer,
and the other, the atheist, in need of work,
as he stood at his window in Warsaw, where it fell
and would keep on falling,
on his youngest, who died in the famine,
on the figures below in their black coats,
on his wife's commodious breasts and hair
every year thinner and longer by an inch—
snow so radiant, it must be the snow
that fell on the shtetl,
and over the farms,
and the fiddlers, and the normal death of infants—

and this is when you came about, Mirenka,
when you suddenly appeared, behind the typewriter,
    white as a bride
  weightless and smiling

a woman, yet young as the day you died,
    first and only sister.

Goat Sister, Chagall bride,
though we may be living in a different painting
sit beside us, tell us what to know—
let us shake up, then enter, your bubble of snow—
as if we have never been lost in history.

Deep, deeper than the
        mothers of snow
there lies a river
        warmer than diamonds
and we sit outside it,
everyone I know—

we are sitting and staring into the snow.

That dark golden Jewish light

that amber light
where Hasidim danced like bells

bells, bells, they rang
lifting elbows and knees
snapping their fingers
Gohtenyu, Gohtenyu
joy be to you!—

in their black suits
emptying their sweaty suits of flesh
their highest fingertips touching G-d
in the fine black night, Gohtenyu,
hear the ringing of a Jew!
as he pivots and swirls
his coat-tails awhirl
before the seated, starry-eyed girls.

Already the village was fragrant with Sabbath.
In the time when elsewhere flesh burned,
like elves they danced,
practical souls,
spinning gold in the darkest night,
whirling shadows in the golden light—

I have been lost in an image forest

so deep that even owls
sit dazed by the moon, whose evidence
streaks across like animal light
in a long, low, illuminating cry—
a forest spilled in the moon's eye
a lost-and-found where the evident is curable.
And my private pathways glisten
and wind, and wind and glisten.
Pathways, a web of silver, I know each
as well as this hour of night
when ghosts become as touchable as
those who have never been lost are not.

A View From The Ghetto
Or, On Either Side

Here I stand at the edge of the field.
Before me wildflowers.
Behind me, dark children
like myself. In the pure spaces
between knotted wire, far off, I see
bits of clothing fluttering
toward us. Nearer.
Behind me, they are staring, some
go home. Others swallow.
Brushing wildflowers they come
closer, picking up stones.
The sun shines on them
Mama? I am running, running. Away from
their blue shirts like the sky,
their hair like the wheat,
their mended dresses ripped by sunlight,
spitting, cursing.
Down the curb, around walls.
Day after day.
Until we are gone.
All the dark ones are gone.
They have no one.

So Many Parades, Mirenka
In memory of 1942

I

Take a deep breath with me, and rest.
We live on an island in the West.
We live on an island on the Left
opposite the one on the Right,
where they shot them into ready graves.

Thinking: those who must fall, have already fallen,
we who are left turn over and over
to face the light that burns in the sky,
our children dancing among flowers and smoke.

From the jailed street, through the town,
to the edge of a field sprinkled with clover,
they walked, slowly, without a word.
Let us join them, slowly, without a word.
Out of their houses the Towns People come
shielding their eyes against the sunset,
the anonymous dirt in God's own eye.

II

One tenth must live, nine tenths must die
and the man must choose who will live or die—
the man at the end of the line
who is sending each of us Left or Right.
He must be standing on something higher,
I can see him even from here, Mama.
Mama, there are no pupils in his eyes.

I don't think *we*'ll die, do you, Mama?
We are different, *we* won't die.... Mama?
The Towns People open and close their mouths.

Suddenly they recognize this mother and child,
the freckles that come to the surface in the light:
the doctor, the barber and his freckled wife—
The People are cheering, the People are not.
The People don't know what it is
they have always wanted.

They have come to the edge of the street
to see, that the street is no longer theirs.
This happens once in a lifetime, this.

III

A few have come from the nearby farms,
where they ate and slept and punished each other.
Summers and winters had turned them out
and the new blown dust in the chicken yard
and the yellow flowers in the fields everywhere.

The dirt was marched from between their eyes
and it all settled into fragrant silence.

Everything that happens, passes in silence.
And the silence blows
the flowers into dancing—look,
they dance even now,
as you stand here, looking around.

Sigh with me, and rest.
We live on an island in the West.
We live on an island on the Left
opposite an island on the Right,
where they stand digging their graves.

Glass Beaded Rings

When my mother told me we were leaving the Ghetto—
shrunken to one tenth since the last Selection—
that we might be safer in a hidden room
in the town prison where my father worked,
I again tried to imagine the place.
                                  Like the Red House
I had hoped I was born in.
I imagined a room with a table and chair, a window with clouds.
I imagined a mother and father, their child in a crib,
the three of us, watching the sunlight come in.

I imagined living without Mrs. Katz
who believed the others were taken to work.
I was weaving glass seed rings with their daughter,
stringing and restringing my glass-beaded rings.
                               Scribbling in the sand, I
assigned myself a number, I don't know why. Number 3,
the fat right side of a woman, a snowman,
a no man... then I added his hat, and his broom.
Around him people with closed eyes
moved over an abyss. But we—
                                    were coming out of the forest,
going to the Red House, I was riding on my father's back,
reaching for the brightest leaves when
suddenly a clearing lit up ahead. In the center
was the prison. I had with me my glass-beaded rings
and I took one from my pocket high into the sun

letting each grain of glass fill up with light.
And when Mama told me we would have to steal
through the town as gentiles, it meant nothing much: I
was a very special number 3, it meant something
must happen only to me. Only to *us*.
                              This isn't to say
that I wasn't afraid, only that I had something
to do. When we came to the edge, come
said my mother. And she tore the yellow off our sleeves.

Light

We live in a prison, Mirenka.
The one called Adam
said, 'We'll manage—if the world
were lit with a single candle
we would all live by that dim light
and the candle? would become the sun.'
But we live in a prison.
When *I'm* free I'll live by
the sun and the moon, not this
lonely beam from the outside
they call 'the light of freedom.'
Only, to escape, someone
must open the gate for me, and
a guard guards the gate,
a giant drunken guard.
They say that sometimes
I sound like a child—but they
only huddle in the pall of this
prison light. I thought
only prisoners were unhappy, but the guards
drink and are unhappy.
They resent us and are so unhappy.
And they are afraid of us.
The Commandant himself
is a child, who never wanted this job of
running a prison, who schemes now
to save us; and he
is the saddest and dearest
bad man in the prison. He actually
let us see him cry. Yes he is the one
who cries. And brings us oranges and Easter eggs.

While the sick lightbulb wanes to the sound of
evening gunfire. Oh evening, the dying
of all light except for this bulb
hanging from the dead center
of the room. In tuberculin light
two black eyes sparkle
and they are the windows.
Those two views of darkness more alive
than the light we live by.

The Prison As A Gray Box

There is something you refuse to recognize:
the guard at the gate is human.
You raised him to be the guard
and he stands there being human.

> *We don't like his stupidity,*
> *his red nose.*

But it's your alcohol that made him drunk.
And the orders he gets are not God's.

> *The problem is how to persuade him,*
> *whisper in his ear that*
> *WE own certain passes*
> *and WE are allowed*
> *to just - walk out.*

Your thoughts will make him cheerful.

You refuse to understand him:
he is, above all, responsible, this guard.
He won't hear your fantastic arguments,
as if you would really take him
on the back of your magic bird,
like the one in his bedtime stories.
He knows you want to trick him,
just because he is a little drunk,
because he dreams a little.

*How stupid it seems, to be circling
around his dilemma, around and around
the prison yard, as the light dies.
And all because of the bulldog at the gate.
No one else, not a soul is in sight.
A group of us, say five, could subdue
the idiot among us, regardless of his size.
At least it seems seemly to discuss it.*

All night the tightening silence
condenses into action—there is not enough time
in the hand of the killer, time compresses
to a weapon forged by the very air, so sharp.
The weapon is brought to his throat, as the guard
laughs unsuspecting, talking about his health,
the way his heart, for instance,
fails him sometimes.

Then there is silence.
Then we are afraid.

Balalaika

These are no gypsy ears
that hear the fire of what might have been
or wolves roaming
in the shadow of a tambourine.
This is no gold that cuts circles of moonlight
under a lobe and shines in the wind
of singers. This is your eye.

This is no gypsy camp
that huddles in the cold;
no song, that throws singing to the dogs;
no hour that whirls without wings
sleeping so
untunicked and unpainted.
This is your cool lip.

This is no balalaika
that wakes the shivering owl
and plucks remembered things:
red cloth, white windy sleeves,
stories that slow the stars
and rock the moon in an iron pot;
under the rushing stars this is
no gypsy night
that hides dancers in a darkening wood.

Joseph's Ark

When Joseph made the flood
he began to understand the god believers believed in,
funny. After all, their lives depended on it,
his wife's and child's, and even his own. They were
going to be shipped out with the others, he had to be extremely
needed, so he stuffed rags here & there in the pipes
across the prison yard, and made rain, hah!
The showers, the faucets! His own rain of laughter.
How funny the human race is, you can't imagine.
The barber! The barber! *Friezer!* they cried. The barber,
the plumber, the manager of the *proviant!* Go get the barber!

How could you let the man do everything? Who can replace him!
screamed the Gestapo. Because, naturally, only Joseph
knew how to fix the flood. And so they remained,
for another month.

How can you let God do everything? Who will replace him!
laughed Joseph. And God, too, stayed another month.

And The Airplanes Fly

We too are cold, Mirenka.
We too sit in a corner
Though it's April.

And the airplanes drone over us
Flying through darkness
Decades, days.

Pilots are dying, everyone dies
And the airplanes fly.

There must be great commerce in the universe,
Tanks are coming from the mouth of God!—

Heaven is an indestructible fortress
We rise daily and daily die

And the airplanes fly.

The Trains

When I was a very small child I wrote a happy poem.

The Trains are Coming! The Trains are Coming!

was its refrain.

The Children are Running! The Trains are Coming!

It had many verses, in Polish, about you can guess what. The trains. I don't remember what the fuss was about. The trains. So what. When I was a child they whizzed by like parties and lemonade, I suppose.

The Trains are Coming! The Trains are Coming!

Also I was that kind of child. Who else would write poems about trains. I was so eager, I wanted to step into every beautiful light. You can imagine the power of a day, the light of day. And in it myself turning and turning. And turning.

The Trains are Coming! The Trains are Coming!

Then, when I was about eight, a train came to load us and carry us to Buchenwald. It stood waiting with four black stomachs; and where were the children? What happened to the children? My mother gave me a cup and told me to walk away forever, as if I was going for a drink of water at the well. I remember walking away from my parents, and who knows what else.

The Trains are Coming! The Trains are Coming!

In Hiding
For the year in hiding with Maria Szumska

Once, in hiding, we went open-
riding in a lenient sleigh
buoyant on the lack of sound and motion
full-away from war
sleepweaving through a back country
my white-haired lady saint and I
our frozen faces craning
from the homespun color:
one soft hour the sound of bells was all.
We were missed by the storm
in its silent eye:
mounds of forest meandered past us
and clearer, closer intrusions
fled like calendars behind
their knowledge of our presence—
nature had to wait, we folded leaves
to dream in our escape, the sleigh
was like a god-crib carried by
some fabled beast across her snowy haven
and it hazed the deep green to a waiting green
where animals we knew of kindly
slept unblessed. Our war went still
and deep, around the weightless sleigh.
And in a trembling present,
tense with the lunacy of peace
such as it is, a masquerade in blooming
shades of sacrifice, of comfort jaws
of love-drops like the red of war—

I crane my turtle-head for frozen air,
or, burrowing into
the soft escape, the open ride,
I hear, beside the child I was,
those constant
bells pulling
our phantom sleigh.

Haloes

There were none like Mary's.
Jesus', majestic,
ringed his head with power,
  a hot white ember in the dark.
  Mary's halo made a dust of bombs,
even of the sounds of the airplanes
that carried them—no beastly
second coming, no war, no
    mother and father gone. Bombs fell
and we sat under a tree, her namesake and I,
        eating apples.

  Haloes are the soft lights
we put around people we love,
are the awesome rings of light
  around people we fear,
who are unexplainable.

  In the cabin, alone, the haloes on
the three walls gave off a soundless
hum, a light converging at the center
    of the room, which was silence
more mysterious than evil.
      Who could fathom the shadows?
      Who could fathom the haloes?

   The kerosene lamp flickered
and it smelled of *real*-kerosene, the flame
wavering like *souls* I'd read about,
          threatening to *go out*.

Honest and true kerosene lamp,
honest and true chickens in the empty
fireplace, flying up without warning, shrieking
like the devil's hands. Real and
 true chickens, but were they?
Blessed honey of haloes,

their light spreading when I was
afraid. I found them in the Book,
I found them on the walls, on the
three Jesuses, and the one large benevolent
Mary, the child in her arms
     a real child.

   No daylight could match the
light of the haloes in the tightly bolted
cabin—only, in the window, much, much
        later, perhaps, the holy moon.

Joseph On The Night Of Nights
1943: A parachute lands in a tree in the Underground at midnight, dropping provisions.

                                 …then
he opens his eyes, is once more
in the dugout, camouflaged
by branches, removes them, poking
upward—a night of angel snow, hah!
But irony doesn't change a thing,
the woods are gentled by falling snow,
as if defeating the war—and he rises,
steps onto cold earth, clears
branches away, and emerges.
      As a child he knew
this; it is not the world.
Snow like a mother floating
lazily down? The walkers, the others,
are they sleepwalkers? Why
and where are they going?
          Ah… look, white in all
the trees, and the plane humming
away, and the young girl, Mania?
laughing as she runs: Meat!
Meat! they cry. Coffee! Coffee?
What kind of dream is this?
A pocket knife, look! And Stefan
   a big man like Stefan
is crying. *Things!* And Kolya,
hugging himself, and Masha
rocking the ghost of her baby.
     And still the snow like a fable
the warm, crazy snow, has it come
all this way from old Warsaw? is it
memory snow? He would scream
but now they are running to the fire—

soon they will sing about the vanished
boys with ruddy cheeks, with glory
and a piece of cake in their bundles!
He would laugh until morning but
no, snowflakes disguise the darkness,
peacefulness can make a person wild
   can make believers out of saints.
Run, to the other end of the woods,
dig yourself a private hole, turn your face
from this snow-flecked blackness
and *be*, without dreaming, Joseph,
with the night.

The Village Girl's Dream

I love the men of the world and their visions.
I draw their pictures on the whiteness before me
then step through beaded curtains
into their arms.
They throw me over their shoulders
    like knapsacks
and eat their rations out of my heart,
it is my blood that spills from their veins
into new countries.

And I will hold you, child,
I will wrap you in all my aprons
and let you rise slowly
like bread
which doesn't know man from woman.

Habry

Habry, peaceful Polish flowers,
Mine, yet I never belonged to that country.
Fraying, breezing in the quietest quiet,
Blue, all along the edge of the wheatfield,
Silken blue, among orange poppies,
And the sun is silent, silent as the night.

How can so much sunlight sink so quietly?
How can it be that no one is here?
I, after all, have never left that countryside
And not even the Poles are visible, and where
Are the girls who forever wove garlands
And ran through flowers as if they were air?

I return to habry as if by candlelight,
Warmed, though I know they are nowhere near,
There is nothing like them in poor Illinois,
No Jews-and-gentiles, nothing to separate
Petal from petal - only hushed blue
Habry, hovering in the air.

Praised by your name, no one.
For your sake
we shall flower.
Towards
you.
                     — Paul Celan (tr. Michael Hamburger)

I remember coming into Warsaw, a child

out of a sheer, sunlit countryside,
where sometimes a goat made the only sound in
all the universe, and a car engine would certainly
tear the wing of an angel. Entering burnt Warsaw
and the Sound of the World, how strange, how lonely
the separate notes of Everything, lost in a smell of
spent shots still smoking, a ghost of bombs, a silence
of so many voices, the ruined city singing not only
a post-war song but an Everything hymn of dogs wailing,
a car, a horse, a droning plane, a slow, distant
demolition, hammers like rain, the hum, the hum,
bells and levers and voices leveled and absorbed
into the infinite hum in which the ruins
sat empty and low like well-behaved children,
the ruins, their holes, like eyes, secretly open,
passing on either side, as we entered Warsaw, an air
of lost worlds in a smoky sweet light ghosting
and willing their sounding and resounding remains

The Children Of War Smile And Are Happy
For the Immigrants of 1947

They buy Happy Buttons at every bazaar
and walk like excellent citizens
in smart little suits,
you might notice one tipping his little hat
and pointing at the sun. They'll eat
most anything. Especially the spicy, meaty, sharp
things that make you cry. Eat, Eat! they implore,
the holes in their mouths replaced with
American gold.

I am reading in a shabby book
about something which doesn't concern me
how some, the dark ones, begged in the streets—
they make me sick, they have no right to
carry such bricks of wisdom around,
they have no class, no dignity
and it's walking naked
to be pleading with the eyes of
the almighty firmament!

Like rats, they shun light.
How can we unteach such educated minds?
How make presentable such black tarnishings?
My pores open their little Ghettoes,
my blood opens the sewers of their survival,
it is impossible to hide them without a stink,
the war is still on, they breathe,
yes the war is still on…

But the children of war smile and are happy.
In pretty boxes they carry gumdrops of
every American memory, pink & blue & purple & red & white
colors from a smiling factory where no one, no matter how
foolish or wise, has ever been, or ever will be
a child of war. But where every modern person

is a child of Archie… Veronica… Batman…
This is what gives their children joy.

To life! they raise their American glasses.
There is no gold rolling in the streets,
no oranges hang from the trees of heaven,
but there is this: to live. Sure,
life may be a small thing, when you think
of all the large things sacrificed to it,
a story unwritten, another in the hands of the illiterate,
or even the dream of oranges.

But the children of war smile and are happy.

Sing Illinois

How easy it was to write American poems,
to sit in school with the May-windows open
and sing Illinois anthems. *O'er the river   gently flowing*
To eat soft, white sandwiches... *Illinois Illinois*
Lose my accent and walk and talk like
Lois Lane. We lived in Texas
for a while, and I talked like a Texan.

But there was another, an older someone,
who had burrowed into the center of the earth
and come out at the other end of the world,
and she packed her bags and is sailing my way…

Her ship comes closer every decade, every minute,
the air begins to ripple tensely, like an ocean
One must lie down quietly and stare at the ceiling.

It takes courage to accept her foreignness.
Here, off the sea, comes the one I must love,
regardless of what country she was born in.

A Jew is a gypsy bird among gypsies.
How can she belong to the country
when the country she belongs to isn't hers?
I was born less in Poland than I was to my parents
and they to the War, which owned them
like a snakeskin that had left its reason.
And no matter how many faces I try on
the new one doesn't fit any better than the old one,
the little one inside me, gray as a fossil,
keeps crying, Where are we? Who am I?

He carried my books in May sunlight,
a boy, when I came to Illinois, America.
They bought me a pink robe, a family, I sank
into their sofas   *O'er the river   gently flo - oh - ing?*

But parents are too powerful a country.
All other countries lie down beside it,
are gardens of prairie and cornfields and flowers,
I live among gentle, deciduous pirates… *Illinois*
And then, she comes on her ship to remind me,
bearing her gift—astonishment—
comes to subdue me.
                    And I stand up.
Oh I was ambitious, I wanted to love less
than my true gods.

The War Gave Birth To Me

The war gave birth to me.
Oh how it labored and labored, Mama.
I don't know what I was thinking of.
Inside it was so gray and dark.
How does it feel now, better?—
now that the thing is out walking
the blossoming streets in the little suburb
naming the honey-blue clouds?
What a heavenly blanket
covers the emptiness, where the war was.
The umbrellas of May.

O where in the month of May
did you put the little gray Jew, Mama?
In sweet, sweet Illinois, child.
Down under, mulching the roses.
The one who escaped and became American?
He sleeps between the meadows and cities.

The war gave birth to me.
Oh how it labored and labored, Mama.
How can it be that it still is?
And what, tell me, has it made of you?
Neither man nor woman, only the child
I am circling and circling, the missing child.

Shh… let us hide in the barn, Yanek,
we can watch the houses go up in flames,
and when it is over, Mary and Yanku,
someone will give us our proper names.

The war gave birth to me, Mama.
I had nothing to say,
I could only stand and watch
overhead
in the Mayberry blue
the oncoming planes,
until finally
I was born a Jew.

My Mother's Roots

My mother

never taught me to embroider
coarse white tunics
            or weave
garlands of warm chamomile,
never took me to circle dances,
never finished a song, or even a phrase,
never sang, but hummed to herself
hummed and hummed
an entire village
cooked and hummed and the humming

was the sound of the world in darkness

was her own mother humming the beginning
of *Enchanted Fairy Tales, Exquisite Fairy Tales*

her mother like a thick white star come out of the night
to touch her, where she stood sweating, tasting the chicken soup
in the middle of the universe
of a house that would not come together

even as turnips and parsnips awakened
the town, the night the first one went, age two,
her hair black as pearls, humming, halo of pearls, turnips,
humming the soup throughout the house

Aleph, *Bet*, humming, A, B, humming, *offen pripechik*, close by the hearth,
where the rabbi stood instructing the children

as if the gentle white scum, carefully removed, would release
the soup to fragrance and heal the
what and the who can say, when was it
she stopped wearing aprons?,

as if the soft steam on the windows
between here & there
were not the steam of a fading locomotive and not
her sisters' breath, celery and carrots
and parsley root – and the leek,
as she smelled it, took up the humming
when I was twelve, then forty, then now,
only a child of the future, not of her home town, not
of the body of the first house where 20 children
were born and died of natural causes while everyone cooked and some
even danced and sang out loud, loud and
haughty in satin and manicured. My
mother's manicured hands
stir, stir & cook, stir

as if she were not dissolving with each
onion, each carrot. She looks at me and smiles and the bits
of humming resume, when was it
I refused to eat her soup?

as if when I sweated to
Russian balalaikas she was not in the shadows to
counterpoint - dancing? dancing?? to steam sweetening and
saddening (she hummed) all the
children behind the walls, the children behind the walls? - whatever
happened to the Russian balalaikas?

She hummed. And the
world changed and changed.
Became. Darkened a shade.
Became the world. Or had been
all along. Ask a thousand
mothers who hum, a million.
In Kenya. In the Andes. In Spain.

As if the chalk circle around my feet,
out of which and into which I jumped
with all the children in the world were not
a house breathing a cloying mist

and I wasn't cooking carrots & parsnips & turnips
& onions & celery & chicken & parsley & salt & pepper & sometimes
parsley root, when I could get it, and the vapors
didn't replenish the night
or soften the stars, as I skimmed
the delicate scum, carefully, when was it
I stopped wearing aprons?

There Are Men

There are men who tell you
to go left or right
when right means death
and left means life.
There are men who tell you
what is black and white.
There are men who tell you
to marry or not.
There are men standing
higher than you are,
with a raised hand and immaculate eyes.
There are winds in the air
in the shapes of men,
there are voices in the house
that take your belief,
there are leaders
who take your belief and spine,
and even if they don't—
there are men who will tell you
to go left or right:
they are waiting in line
even after you die.

And so it is better to sit
absolutely still
in the subway, to the end of the line,
it is better to fold your hands
without prayer,
like a charred-
white tree
about to be cut down.

If you do, nothing will happen,
the cutters too will fold
their hands and sit
in the mausoleum of time
and no one will paint us,
no one will write poems
about us, there will be
no Grecian urns, there will be
only this place,
and our rightful silence.

Drifting Towards You, Malina

I woke up
and the world was changed.
Twice? Three times?
It was when exhaustion, sinking sweeter than desire,
carried you straight to heaven
and later I grew wings
through sheer work and confusion—
there is more disorder, Malina, in
trying to bring order out of chaos
than words can tell,

naked babes.
I was still kicking inside our mother
when you died,
aged two.

I woke up and the world was changed,
the bloody ball burst
and I followed our mother to another place.
        Gray.
She lived there for a long, long time
and then she too died.
Twice? Three times?
I woke up
motherless of course.
The mother room, the mother hour
the mother block and neighborhood,
you know there's no such thing, little sister,

when you move from one shadow to another
and now in tangerine autumn
      the fruity sweetness in the air   uncertain:

My sister loves me,
is smiling at me this very moment,
ageless as a raspberry on ice,
a raspberry.   Your name: Malina.

A timeless sweetness on the tongue.
If I were very young again,
then what?

You grow back, like a leaf
in spring. You loved me then, even at two,
me, silent and unborn, heard me saying
the things I still say,
unsettled as an unmade bed,
were gone.
Lived in with us.

I woke up
and the world was changed.
Was open, screamed open
its blood-light,
the act of seeing like a wound suddenly
no longer red,
Malina
already a speaking thing
already a non-being
a writing in my mouth
    alive
I swallowed into words.

I woke up drifting towards you,
Malina,
out of a long
wake
and you let me sleep.

Among The Unsurvived

Sometimes the whispering in the sky
  is so loud, that on earth
  the stock market falls
    down & up
    down & up like a heartbeat.
A thousand mosquitoes
  are biting at the heart
        There? Here?
There is no more separation
no more notions of destiny,
we eat and the whispering ebbs
we sleep and the whispering flows.
It is, as if with our lives
we conduct the insect music on high,
  their monotonous gossip.
Who married whom; the price of oranges.

Of course they can hear other worlds
moving in and out of the universe
  but we are family
  we are their organs
  their earthly swelling
  there is nothing if not blood here—

Suddenly I wake up naked
feeling my grandmother's breath on me.

Sometimes the whispering is so loud,
I wake up in the middle of the night
to lie still and listen
as a bare tree listens to its leaves.

It is said that when the world ends
there will be silence
no one will speak through us
there will be nothing to speak through
all these dressers and tables and sofas
not to mention the flutes and pianos
and harps.

And is this why
tenors sing and shepherds pipe,
why time moves backwards and forwards?
My own head hums,
I open my summer window to the soft percussion
of insect lovers, the clatter of trains,
rain, the rumble of future rain.

Above all, the whispering up there.

Retirement Village

The golden land of my parents
floating away, away. Golden,
Golden Lakes Village.
The moon passes slowly over it.
Low, full, sensual moon.
Farther each day.
People on slow bicycles;
trees, breezes at the end of a dream.
The river soft as a dream.
Winding among brown houses,
mirroring unrippled, silent
as the low, damp moon.
A man passes by slowly
in white pants, a lanolin look.
His jokes around the swimming pool
blow into the sunset.
No one should die here. The trees
clipped, the pool warm and blue,
the driveways painted orange,
the little doorways, the blossoming trees.
The tennis courts, the clubhouse,
the cigar-lit pool and game room.
Sun-browned women,
men in creamy sweaters
under umbrellas. Fountains.
No one should be ill here.
How I long for you,
silver moon passing
in my mother's and father's window.
Dear Florida, silent and sensual.
They move in a golden state,
away, away. Calling.

People Look In

People look in.
All the little boxes—
All the little houses
All the little days.
Some people look in.
Bending down down low
Taking courage
Some people try, on good days.
Taking the time.
Looking for the
Woman who lived in a shoe
The little man on his little chair
In his little room.
Some people finally hold
The little room
In the palm of a hand
And bend down down low
To look. Taking heart.
Some people, sometimes.
On a good day.
All the little boxes
All the little men, and women
On their little chairs,
In the palm of a hand.
And the boxes blossom
like flower boxes.
This is all there is.

My Mother's Dishes

My mother the breeze
arose one day
out of an earth of wishes.
She bloomed, a serious orange rose,
yielding to the garden
all her dishes—

locked in a worn-out
blonde buffet. To get them
she bends deeply.... reaches…
"I thought I had another one like that,
you look."
The things she's saved.
Relish trays, odd saucers, pitchers,
jars, bottoms of butter dishes.
Platters in plastic zipped bags.
"That one." We pull it
from the middle of a stack.

          My almost
vanished mother's dishes. Soon I
will feel among glass, brass, porcelain,
saucers from when I was fifteen,
chipped, cheap, gold-rimmed dinner plates
floating a beige stalk of wheat.

And will you stand behind me,
as I stand behind her,
you, staring with me at the ragged carpet,
the bedspread (will you say it?) that not so long ago

covered them turning transparent and quietly
carrying themselves away?

Will you stand behind me when I turn—
"Here is the one
you took for the carrot cake
last time when Joanna came to visit"—

remembering with me that close to the end
everything she cooked tasted the same?
The soup, the carrot cake, bland, reheated.
"Everything tastes good to me," she smiled,
saltless, sharpless, suddenly harmless.

And with every step, as I walk out with her,
will I too give up memory, flesh, skin?

Her gauzy eyes widen, wider,
sheer, unshuttered, letting the breeze through.
She has stopped, to recall a sentence she'd begun,
and we walk on, and the sun shines through her

as though to sweep out her "ripe old age,"
her sad smile finally solidified—
but wait, Joanna is still coming,
we are pulling out all the good dishes,
the cordial glasses for Blackberry Brandy
"and Helen, go, look for the cards!"

My minikin father trudges in
dragging his broken shoulder behind him.
"Nobody heals as fast as me!" And
"I used to be real good-looking, look!"
A picture trembles out of his pocket.
"Just like my daughter!"
I am twenty-one.

He bends over the ghost of food,
cutting, slicing, carrying the knife
across their village of slow motion.
Bends over a hallowed orange,
shuffles to the window to look at the neighbors—
returns to the ritual of garlic and rice.
My father, entirely consumed by food.

I remember the contempt I once had
first for the old, then for the young.
Then for myself.

Poor dishes. Clattering away.
In the twilight of a future rummage sale, dishes.
Prehistoric dishes.
Bone of my bone.

My mother's sheer flesh, beaming,
carries the dishes for whoever's coming.
And the room flutters
with future meaning.

My mother's dishes.
Her potato kugel, her barley soup,
her blue sofa, my mother's skin.
On the wall, her Monday night paintings.

> *My mother the breeze*
> *arose one day*
> *out of an earth of wishes.*
> *She bloomed, a serious orange rose,*
> *yielding to the garden*
> *all her dishes—*

When You Finally Marry

When you finally marry your mother
never mind the myth and symbols, of land, arbors,
milkmaids prettying the fields—

Here she comes, down the steps,
carefully, and enters your soul.
You stare at her.

Poke her like a rubber doll
down into
her jack-in-the box.

Pop, there she is!
Holy binoculars! Is this her life?
Is this what marriage is about?

***

When you finally marry your father
he rushes in grinning like a bear
who will never dance
but instead walks around mixing cocktails.
Blue drinks.
Red drinks.
Who are you, daddy?
Finally you marry the who-are-you
and let him have a good-old-time.
Let him sit in the bathroom for hours
reading Michener, shaving and perfuming up.

The man who made you
jump in the pool and swim.
The man who never made you
do anything but swim.
O daddy, daddy, make me good,
make me crimson with laughter and evil,
make me a woman.
He sits there watching TV.
Civilized man. A beer in his hand.
Climbs up to bed, climbs down for
an aspirin.
God of mythology, voodoo man.
Master of thirty magenta concubines.
Lover of war and corpses.
Who are you daddy?
Honking your red hot horn at other cars.

Decoder of stock markets,
holy scriptures made into daily bread.
O give us. Daddy in your chair.
Daddy in the blue light of the screen,
after the anthem, after the images.
Daddy in the wee hours.

When I married my first father,
I was in love.
We murdered the fat mother in my soul.
It was a beautiful day,
each day my first son was born,
each day my first moonlike daughter
rose like an archetypal symbol.
Zeus shot his diamond arrows,
Innana descended into hell and was saved.

We shed children, like blossoms, in our wake,
they faded into the world and
grew into something else.

When I married my second father,
it was when everyone was writing poems
to appease the self and not the soul.
My mother stood outside, quietly
as if we lived in a palace.
Small as a child,
a rose in her hand.
Looking up.
                    O vanity.
Orange, purple and gold.
How smooth and satin you are.
He and I, we made a bed of
poetry to lie on.
God of skin, God of recognition.

When I married my third father
I was reading that essay by Donald Hall.
Work on the book, he said.
Pay with thyself as coin.
I heard the jangling of a purseful.
Under the bed. On
top of which he wanted
to make love to me. No, that
isn't the word. Release.
The way a tree fades in October.
Lantern; orgasm. Silence.

Autumn is all I know of spring.
Summers I sit on a chaise-lounge, longing.
Summer, the season of what ought to be.
He said, work on the book.
The book? The book.

We went downtown to the movies,
worked on a five year plan,
brought home The Quiet Man,
climbed into bed, and watched TV.
Words popped like bubbles out of soda.
We threw peanuts at the bears.

When I finally married my mother,
I noticed myself, I came away
from myself. Since to marry anyone
is to leave them forever in the box
they want to remember as paradise.

The air turned into onions and carrots,
a chicken squirmed in her arms.
Steam, not mist.
Work & worry.
Not lanterns in October.
Not the daisylike sun
in a child's painting.

The sun warms the walls with such
fleeting transparencies.

And it isn't whether you get it or not,
it's what you want that counts,
the image of

an incandescent bride and bridegroom
    as if rising out of water

Lord & Lady, help the unresolved,
    keep giving birth to us,
        simple as we are.
My father who will never dream,
my mother who will never dance,
how gracefully they touch and change places
    and we look up.

How You Saved My Life
For The Hidden Child group - Chicago

You were frightened,
    your eyes like murder.
And *you,* cemented down
    to your bowels
And it was all about tomorrow
    and what death looked like,
  would it take your child—
    who was a little strange
    but a wonder—
  the evening darker than a field of
        cabbages
    and memory gone
  beneath the squeeze of fear—
      tomorrow—
You were frightened,
    your face on the floor.
And *you,* thrashing, thrashing,
  you could have plowed a thousand
        fields
  with such wildness,
But you were my parents, and you let me go.

To Keep My Mother Happy

To keep my mother happy, I would buy her a kitchen.
It could be in the middle of nowhere, a meadow, the universe,
she would stand there in the middle of the emptiness
cutting leeks, carrots, chicken and asking about
the children are the children all right? tell me—
I would get her a big refrigerator. Big. Big enough
for buckets of soup, kugels the size of giftboxes,
oranges and grapefruits the size of Florida. And
room for moving around, humming, telling you what to do:
It's a crazy world. Take a look at yourself.
I would get her a big bus for the garbage, a gigantic
cutting board, a chopper oh boy, and a wooden bowl.
It's a crazy world without a chopper.
People go to restaurants and eat and eat.
But into her kitchen would come the hungrier than
hungry, and out of her kitchen a mighty sleep, cosmic and
awesome, her voice still echoing... Do you like it? Is it good?

Flowers may grow into trees and trees into planets and planets
to steel and steel to some unnamable glory, something
known and recorded and filed, and restored into
flowers again, and she wouldn't notice,
she would have her kitchen.
No walls, no floor, no ceiling, just a little kitchen.

Only, I would make it big.

The Faces, Up There

I think of my parents, who died naturally.
I think of all the movie stars with them.
Are they forced to mingle?
I think of Helen Vendler, who will
follow me up to heaven one day.
She'll say to me, looking down,
look at them, still coming, a steady stream
of poets, would be poets, great poets,
closet poets and poets without a clue.
And who will be the next I to judge them
as we are judged in this - blue?
She will look around at the brilliance
of heaven, its uncanny intelligence
of light, and then see my parents,
eternal immigrants
still holding on by the elbows,
still looking around suspiciously,
beside Bogie and Helen Hayes and,
in another corner entirely, the faceless,
all with the same face, who came up
merely as smoke and were given the
face of God

and everyone will look away from them,
for how can one look at so much holiness,
and they will be alone, once again,
even in heaven.

And I will stand there staring
through the eyes of Cary and Judy and Frank, because
soon we will all be there, trailing
our little eternities, populating every inch
of the galaxies and the cities between
the stars.

And there will be Jane Eyre, and
there, The Man with the Iron Mask, and all
the Lilliputians, and of course Sisyphus,
for heaven loves the struggle and the brave
faces of fiction, and no one
no one will look upon the holy, for
the face of the holy is ashes and smoke.

It's been centuries

        since my parents died.
        We know this isn't true
        and yet you don't doubt me.
        You know how everything important
        is history by the time your shoes are tied

        that you live in a land of failed imagery
        as if you were not broken enough.
        In Israel an Arab singer dies
        in yellow and reds, her song soaked
        in desert blood, an Arab Arab
        or a Jewish one, who cares
        beneath the exotic sun.
        There's talk of war again.
                                              In Pakistan by now
        perhaps the yellow is tan,
        in Russia, gold, in India, gilded or turn them around
        and everywhere poetry is written in blood
        while we dream our dreams of a blue universe

        our dogs picking at ground zero.
        It's been centuries since my parents died

        back into their war-torn time
        and behind that, childhood
                                    quietly bleeding
        in their last bodies flung across the bed
        like two angry, ragged dolls.
        You'll understand that I'm sucking on
        a gray lollipop, a sugar of dust,
        a sooty snow sculpture gone by dusk.
        There's talk of war again.

In a poor country
death glows in the bones
of quaint children who won't cry out
at our noise.

Every country is a poor country.

The Return of Rhyme

Fall is an Audenesque season.
One drives through it reminded of
ruins, richly transcending.
Of perennial things, as things are ending.

Like the copper oak in a passing cemetery
or ahead, through a brooding mist of rain,
the drenched paper orange of trees,
baroquely opaque, about to be seized—

recurring shapes the wind chips away.
Like a dancer, who disregards as she whirls
her own relics of glass and clay,
which attend her, but also get in her way—

Revealed as if by a stupor of the season,
she dances on, past rhyme or reason.

She looked among her friends

and in fairy tales, between diamonds
of sun in a black forest and in
her hair, and among the clouds with their
open faces, she looked between the winking
minutes on the playground, between hours
of learning heavy as books, she removed their
bookmarks and looked between the pages through
their eyes, and between the pumpkins at a
pumpkin stand, and among the rising voices
of her children, and the secret markings
on public walls, and in offices, more
than anywhere in offices, among the wise,
and when driving she looked into other vehicles
for it, and even when she slept, where all
was silence and protean darkness, and the looking
was like playing the scales, playing with the scales,
and she looked between her old alphabet blocks
still rising into towering complexities…
in cities, in the parks, in all the countries she
wished she had lived in, and it was never
there, never quite there, and the looking
became a habit, like opening windows and
calling her friends, it became simply
looking, the way she had looked for berries
in a forest, or seashells, something
ordinary, even pebbles, anything natural and
slightly different, itself, simply
looking; and then, one day, she found it in
her hands, and never knew how
it had come into her hands, nor what
it was, really.

The Writer

The Poor Still Sing and Dance
The Cold Still Warm the Heart

Is it known to you
that the moment you lie down
your father stands up in your hand?
No? You had gentle parents.
Mine were born with the fire of creation
coiled inside out, two long residues of fire
joined by their forked tongues of love.
Like bleeding rock, like vagrant veins of lava,
they must have longed to have been
cooled off, assimilated into
a single, clean, civilized shape,
a cockle shell in a nursery rhyme,
a plastic bride-and-groom on a cake.
Hot, they poured into each other
and, I outside them, froze in the shade.

Now, finally gone, they sit
and rock in their white on white
no longer sepia
rocking chairs up there,
neutral as a pair of paper doves,
shmoozing me down, yawning
straight down through a cloud,
Have you ever thought, Halinka, about
how frozen you are? O,
the blind, blind angels.
I shall turn off the blue light of heaven—
I shall lie down
with all the fans on! Since,
don't they know, the moment I lie down,
a fire starts in my hand.

Survivors

My parents survived.
  I survived.
My grandparents and aunts and uncles
were taken up into the sky.
I can see them floating
  up there,
spending their eternity
looking for me:
age five
in a tan little box felt hat
and a smart little suit to match,
all embroidered with red.
A chubby child who loved the park.
You remember? they smile.
They are baking a babka for me
in the sky, stuffing it with
raisins and blueberries
almonds and sugar;
let her have everything, they say,
the whole store, the whole country,
the whole of our lives—
if only we can find her.
And so they keep on looking
  for me and for each other
in the great white fog,
and life goes on, in heaven.

This Morning

This morning I dared to read poems
with breakfast, I mean poems
with a Polish accent,
Zagajewski, laying out the afterbirth
of war onto a book called Canvas,
among the seasons, the passing colors.
And I thought yes, when only yesterday,
reading in the same book, I had thought—no.
And the odors around breakfast dimmed
with relativity. I thought, Anything,
anything, affects the canvas,
this morning, for instance. Coffee
at the right temperature, yesterday's
fear lingering in the coffee, the cooling
of summer, mid-September. And the chill
creeping in the slightly open window
brought up pale sketches of
Billy Collins working to make it all
right, but no. Nothing on the front line,
and I thought of Yeats dreaming of Byzantium,
and Rilke working it out with the angel,
and Stevens laying on another layer of liquid
artifice sung to a Southern wave, and
everyone at play, our simple wooden
building blocks towering, careening,
falling, to the music of whose cry or
was it laughter? And, finished with breakfast,
I ran upstairs into the fog abloom with
outrageously fantastic flowers. Imagine.

The Woman With Many Lines

She says: Now that I have unwound my many hoops
of bony stays and turned to fluid rock,
that I have lost the weight of flesh
from dusty corners in a heavy scent of old blossom,
unwound the rose from its blood-cloth
            starched and carpet-heavy goblet
and its pungent gifts: cooking   steaming
a purple sleep
high to the neck   and its dream
of black-and-white kittens unwinding
hoops of yarn against a warm stove wall,
rings ringing me at wrists and ankles
                loving my joints
calling me Queen or Nymph or Mother of Man—
unwound the hoops of fiery-green pendants
and beads and leaves that burned and engraved
my many hoops
and my mother's pea-green eyes lie
on their sides with courtesans and chimney-sweeps
Now that I have unwound from the proud belle hoops
and done the hunting and the leaping—
the old man, the galloping tyrant
cools and softens my shoes   and says
now the high time is over   let the lines speak

About The Author

Helen Degen Cohen was born Halina Degenfisz in a small town near Warsaw. When the Germans invaded, the family fled to Lida, White Russia, but were eventually incarcerated in the Lida Ghetto by the advancing Germans. Because the Ghetto population was shrinking due to the Selections (people being marched into a field, weeded out and shot), Helen's father found a way of getting the family out of the Ghetto, to live in semi-hiding in the little prison where he worked. When finally all remaining Jews in Lida were to be exported, and the family stood at the train station waiting to board, her mother gave Helen a cup and told her to pretend to be going for water at a pump, and to keep on walking – until she found the house of the prison cook. The cook in turn found a devout Catholic, who hid Helen in a cabin in the farm country. Meanwhile, Helen's parents were forced onto the train with the rest, and later jumped from the train and joined the Partisans (aka the Resistance, or the Underground). They found Helen after the war, eventually made it to a Displaced Persons Camp in West Germany, and later emigrated to the U.S. Since then, the author has lived and raised a family in the Chicago area.

Helen Degen Cohen is the recipient of a National Endowment for the Arts Fellowship in Poetry, an Indiana Writers' Conference Award in Poetry, First Prize in British Stand Magazine's International Short Story Competition, three Illinois Arts Council Literary Awards for fiction and poetry, and an Illinois Arts Council Fellowship. Her work is the subject of scholarly essays, including: "Rootlessness and Alienation in the Poetry of Helen Degen Cohen", by Miriam Dean-Notting (Kenyon College), in *Shofar* (University of Nebraska Press) and "This Dark Poland – Ethnicity in the work of Helen Degen Cohen", by John Guzlowski, in *Something of My Very Own To Say: American Woman Writers of Polish Descent* (Columbia University Press). She has received fellowships to majors arts colonies in the U.S., including Yaddo, The MacDowell Colony, the Virginia Center For Creative Arts, and Ragdale. She was the featured poet twice in the Spoon River Poetry Review.

The author has two bodies of work, one about the war and the other about everything else. Seven sections of her autobiographical novel, The Edge of the Field, have been published to date, the latest in 2009 in "Where We Find Ourselves", an anthology by SUNY. One section received first prize in Stand Magazine's International Competition (England), and another received an Illinois Arts Council Literary Award. The chapbook "On A Good Day One Discovers Another Poet" (2009), falls into the everything else category, and is part of a large collection entitled The Book of (night) Writing. Ms Cohen publishes widely in literary journals such as The Partisan Review, Another Chicago Magazine, The Minnesota Review, Cream City, The Spoon River Poetry Review, Versal (Holland), Stand Magazine (England), The Antigonish Review (Canda), Akcent (Poland), and Nimrod (forthcoming in 2009). She is working on a backlog of manuscripts, including much poetry, short and long fiction, essays, and work for theater and children.

Helen Degen Cohen has traveled statewide as an Artist-In-Education through the Illinois Arts Council, and taught at Roosevelt University. She is a founding and current editor of the poetry journal, Rhino, and coordinates its popular adjunct workshop, The Poetry Forum. Her many loves include painting, the rumba, movies, gardening, the jitterbug, designing book covers, folk dancing, walking in the woods, the New York City Ballet, raspberries, and habry, the blue cornflowers that grew along the edges of wheat fields.

THE PUDDIN'HEAD PRESS

Publisher and distributor of fine books

CURRENT TITLES

ORDINARY by Carol Anderson
THROUGH MY EYES by Samuel Blechman
INSIDE JOB by Robert Boone
HABRY by Helen Degen Cohen
CONVERSATIONS WITH FRIENDLY DEMONS
AND TAINTED SAINTS by Nina Corwin
LAKE MICHIGAN SCROLLS by John Dickson
I'M NOT TONIGHT by Kris Darlington
IMAGING CENTER by Sandy Goldsmith
LADY RUTHERFURD'S CAULIFLOWER by JJ Jameson
BROTHERKEEPER by Larry Janowski
EIGHT DOLLARS AN HOUR by Lee Kitzis
THE LAUNDROMAT GIRL by Lee Kitzis
PROFESSIONAL CEMETERY by Johnny Masiulewicz
SHAPE SHIFTER by Tom Roby
CHICAGO PHOENIX by Cathleen Schandelmeier
LAKE MICHIGAN AND OTHER POEMS by Jared Smith
WHERE IMAGES BECOME IMBUED WITH TIME by Jared Smith
INHERITANCE by Marydale Stewart
PROPHECIES by Lawrence Tyler
THE ANTI-MENSCH ANTHOLOGY
THE ANTI-MENSCH II ANTHOLOGY
STARWALLPAPER STUDENT ANTHOLOGY

Published by Puddin'head Press and Collage Press

THRESHOLDS by Jeff Helgeson
CROWDPLEASER by Marc Smith
LESSONS OF WATER AND THIRST by Richard Fammeree

For more information and a complete catalog contact us:

Puddin'head Press
P. O. Box 477889
Chicago IL 60647
(708) 656-4900
(888) BOOKS-98 (orders only)

www.puddinheadpress.com
phbooks@compuserve.com